YOUNG JIM THORPE
BRIGHT PATH

DON BROWN

ROARING BROOK PRESS
NEW MILFORD, CONNECTICUT

Published by Roaring Brook Press

Roaring Brook Press is a division of Holtzbrinck Publishing Holdings Limited Partnership

143 West Street, New Milford, Connecticut 06776

Distributed in Canada by H. B. Fenn and Company Ltd.

Library of Congress Cataloging-in-Publication Data

Brown, Don, 1949-

Bright path : young Jim Thorpe / Don Brown.—1st ed.

p. cm.

1. Thorpe, Jim, 1887-1953—Juvenile literature.   2. Athletes—United States—Biography—Juvenile literature.

3. Indian athletes—United States—Biography—Juvenile literature.   I. Title.

GV697.T5B76 2006   796'.092—dc22

ISBN-13: 978-1-59643-041-9

ISBN-10: 1-59643-041-9

Roaring Brook Press books are available for special promotions and premiums.

For details contact: Director of Special Markets, Holtzbrinck Publishers.

Photographs on page 39 courtesy of the Cumberland County Historical Society,

Carlisle, PA

First Edition May 2006

Book design by Jennifer Browne

Printed in China

10 9 8 7 6 5 4 3 2 1

For Ron, Amy, Darcie, and Kenny.

Nine-year-old Jim Thorpe trotted the Oklahoma plains hunting raccoons. Yellow, brown, and green grassland seemed to unfurl endlessly in all directions. The land belonged to the Sac and Fox Indians, Jim's tribe. At his birth in 1888, he had been called Wa-tho-huck, which meant Bright Path. In time, Jim Thorpe would be called the World's Greatest Athlete.

Summer or winter, Jim seemed to spend all his time in the open. He hunted, stalking raccoons, tracking deer, or snaring quail in traps made of cornstalks. He played wild games with his friends, too. His favorite was Follow-The-Leader where Jim and the other boys swam rivers, climbed trees, and dashed among the livestock.

But life wasn't all games and hunting. His parents, Hiram and Charlotte, farmed and Jim and his four brothers and sisters helped tend crops, feed livestock, and tame horses.

Despite the hard work, Jim found excitement in his chores.
"At ten I could handle a lasso," he said. "I liked catching wild horses on the range. It was great sport."

If asked, Jim probably would have wished for outdoor days of play and work to unfurl as endlessly as the Oklahoma prairie. But at age six, his parents enrolled him in a school just for Indian children where he'd be taught to act and dress like white people. At that time, many people believed that the Indians' best future lay in pushing aside their culture.

The school forced Jim to wear a dark suit and a black hat, and prohibited him from speaking his Indian language. He followed a rigid schedule, lived in a dormitory, and played only games chosen by the school.

Jim did not like it and often ran away.

Once, it was said, Jim scampered away moments
after being delivered to school by his father, and reached
home before the older man arrived on horseback.

Hoping that a more distant school would discourage his running away, Hiram sent eleven-year-old Jim to another Indian school, far away in Haskell, Kansas. Jim disliked this school, too. Haskell was military strict and the students even wore army-style uniforms. Still, he stole moments of fun playing football with his friends using a crudely sewn leather ball stuffed with rags.

At Haskell, Jim learned that his father had been injured. Without getting permission from the school, he raced for home, hopping a freight train to get there. But the train steamed off in the wrong direction and young Jim had to spend two weeks tramping his way 270 miles back to Oklahoma.

At home, he found his father recovered. But tragedy struck soon afterward when his mother fell ill and died. Hiram was now without the help of his wife, causing Jim to give up school and work the farm with his father. But Hiram was a hard man with a hot temper, and he punished Jim for mistakes or forgotten chores. In 1901, he bullied his son once too often and Jim fled. Young Thorpe, about a hundred pounds and less than five feet tall, was thirteen years old.

He ran away to the Texas Panhandle, where he fixed fences on a ranch and tamed wild horses.

Jim came home a few months later, and presented his father with a team of horses.

For several years afterward, Jim attended a nearby public school and played baseball with his friends on diamonds scratched from abandoned wheat fields.

But Hiram saw an Indian school as the brightest hope for his son's future and placed Jim in one across the country in Carlisle, Pennsylvania. It was 1904.

carlisle

Nearly a thousand Indian girls and boys were enrolled at Carlisle: Sioux, Chippewa, Oneida, Hopi, Inuit. Like Haskell, it was military strict. The boys wore army-style tunics and their long hair was cropped. Students followed an unbending routine of reading, writing, and arithmetic.

Trades were taught too, and Jim—cowboy and tamer of wild horses—found himself studying to be a tailor.

The only real pleasure Jim found was in the pickup baseball and football games after classes.

During the summer, Jim and the other Carlisle students were sometimes hired out to nearby farms. Jim cleaned house and tended to rows of vegetables.

It was glum work and Jim ran away, an offense that landed him for a time in the Carlisle guardhouse; the school had once been a military camp and used the dank room as kind of a jail for wayward boys.

Three years of schooling, tailoring, and hired-out summers passed; his life seemed to be trapped in Carlisle like a quail in a cornstalk snare.

Then, while watching the Carlisle's track team practice one afternoon in 1907, Jim noticed that none of the high jumpers could clear the bar.

"I asked if I might try it," he later said. "I had a pair of overalls on, a hickory shirt, and . . . looked like anything but a high jumper."

While onlookers snickered,
Jim approached the bar . . .
and cleared it on the first
try, breaking the school
high-jump record!

Astonished by Jim's casually achieved feat, Carlisle's coach,
Pop Warner, drafted him onto the school's track team
and soon afterward, the football team. With
Pop's training, Jim blossomed into an
astounding athlete.

By 1912, he'd won track medals for dashes, hurdles, hammer throws, and the shot put, and led a handful of other talented Carlisle athletes to victories over much larger schools. He had also played minor-league baseball in North Carolina, earning a few dollars a game.

Jim and the Carlisle football squad defeated the best college teams of the time: Harvard, Syracuse, Princeton, Nebraska, Minnesota, and Pennsylvania.

On the football field, passes flew from Jim's hand with a snap of the wrist, and he scooped up spinning punts on the dead run. He skidded through defenses, and shook off tacklers. He's a greyhound, spectators declared, a jackrabbit, a dynamo, a steam engine! Catching him was like trying to clutch a shadow, someone said.

Then Jim won a place on a special American track team. In the summer of 1912, he and his teammates sailed to Stockholm, Sweden, where they met athletes from twenty-eight nations competing in the 5th Olympic Games.

Jim entered the pentathlon, a grueling contest of jumping . . .

javelin . . .

as well as a 200-yard sprint . . .

discus throwing . . .

and a race of nearly a mile.

Few of the 30,000 spectators believed he'd succeed. No American was up to the task, they thought. And besides, Thorpe had never competed in a pentathlon before.

Jim surprised the crowd and beat his competitors in four of the five events, winning the gold medal with a score that was never equaled.

And just a week later, Jim challenged the world's most gifted athletes in the decathlon, a ten-event contest more punishing than the pentathlon.

Muscles made nimble and fleet by his hardy Oklahoma childhood and Carlisle sports now found their full strength in the three-day contest.

Jim scored third in the javelin throw and pole vault, and second at discus, long jump, and 100- and 400-meter dashes. He won the high jump, shot put, the long-distance run, and a dash that forced the runners to clear hurdles as they ran.

Jim Thorpe won the decathlon with a score that would stand for twenty years!

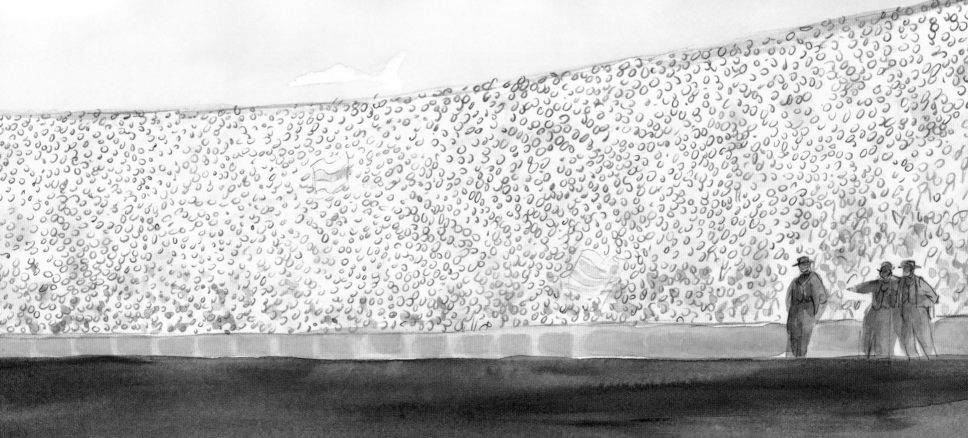

As the onlooking crowd cheered themselves hoarse, perhaps Jim recalled the high jump he had made years earlier at Carlisle. There was something magical about that jump: On one side of the bar Jim had been an Indian boy unhappily struggling in an unfamiliar world, a boy with dim prospects. But on the other side, Jim Thorpe found the bright path to world fame.

"You are the greatest athlete in the world!" the king of Sweden declared as he presented Jim with an Olympic gold medal.

"Thanks, King," Jim replied.

AUTHOR'S NOTE

James Francis Thorpe and his twin brother, Charles, were born May 28, 1888, in a one-room cabin on Sac and Fox land in Indian Territory (now known as Oklahoma). Their mother, Charlotte Vieux, was of Indian, Irish, and French heritage; father Hiram Thorpe was a member of the Sac and Fox Indian nation. Jim's connection to the Sac (Sauk) tribe linked him to Black Hawk, a great Indian leader of the 1830s who battled white settlers, including a young Abraham Lincoln.

The Thorpes had ten children, six of whom would die in childhood, including Jim's twin. The family ranched and farmed on fertile land along the banks of the North Canadian River, producing wheat, cattle, and hogs.

In 1893, six-year-old Jim was sent away to a boarding school for Indians. Special schools for Native Americans had been promoted for centuries, including one opened by Harvard College in 1654. Reformers believed a basic education would allow Indians to join the larger American culture. The Bureau of Indian Affairs, the federal agency administering reservations, began establishing schools in about 1873. Doing so made Indians the only ethnic group in the United States to be provided a well-endowed, government-funded education. Still, Indian education included the dismissal of traditional Native American culture. Indian schools would be central to Jim's life for nearly the next twenty years, first in Oklahoma, then at Haskell, 300 miles away in Lawrence, Kansas, and finally at Carlisle.

The Carlisle Indian Industrial School in eastern Pennsylvania was established at an old army barracks with the backing of the U.S. government. Founder Richard Henry Pratt worked to provide his students with a liberal education, including music and art. Although saying his students should be "thoroughly soaked" in white culture, Pratt didn't share the commonly held belief that Indians were inferior.

Shortly after his arrival, Jim was orphaned: Hiram died of septicemia, or infection of the blood, following his mother, who had died from the same cause in 1901.

By 1907, Jim had been noticed by Glen "Pop" Warner, Carlisle's coach. Warner would eventually become a football legend and is credited with innovations such as the three-point stance, fiber padding for uniforms, the cross body block, and the spiral pass. Warner's Carlisle teams—drawn from only about 250 male students old enough to play—defeated larger schools like Syracuse and University of Pennsylvania.

The 1911 Carlisle football team. Jim Thorpe is in the middle row, third from right; behind him stands coach Pop Warner. The words on the football read: "1911 Indians 18, Harvard 15."

Jim's athletic skills blossomed under Warner. He became the anchor of the Carlisle football team and earned wide attention and admiration. The captain of an opposing team said, "He was superhuman. . . . There is nothing he can't do!" The *Providence Journal* considered him to be "the greatest halfback that ever ranged the gridiron." Jim's speed and strength brought him track and field records for the 100-yard dash, 120 high hurdles, 220 low hurdles, 440- and 1500-yard runs, as well as high jump, pole vault, broad jump, hammer throw, and shot put. Jim also pitched for the baseball team.

In 1909, Jim joined friends and traveled to North Carolina, where he played Class D minor-league baseball for the Rocky Mount Railroaders. The pay, $15 to $25 a week, was more than twice what Jim could earn as a hired hand at farms surrounding Carlisle.

Jim returned to Carlisle and Pop Warner in 1911. That football season saw many Carlisle victories, including an upset over powerhouse Harvard. Jim was voted captain for the next year's team, and was selected for the All-American team, a prestigious award that recognized the best players in the country.

Jim's reputation in track and field, and a special tryout in New York City, earned him a spot on the American team bound for the 1912 Olympics in Stockholm, Sweden. Popular legend has it that Jim never trained during the sea voyage to Sweden—a myth undone by one of his teammates, who remembered Jim running laps and doing calisthenics every day on the ship.

The Games opened on July 6, 1912. The

Jim Thorpe winning the 200-meter dash during the Eastern Olympic Trials at Celtic Park in Queens, New York, in 1911.

pentathlon competition was held the next day. Jim won four of the five events, earning the gold medal. (The winner of the event was the athlete with the lowest score. Jim's 7-point total remained unbeaten when the pentathlon was retired from the Olympics in 1928.)

The 1912 Stockhom Olympics: Jim Thorpe putting the shot.

In subsequent open events, Jim was less successful, placing fourth in the high jump and seventh in the long jump. But on July 13, Jim and twenty-eight other athletes began the three-day, ten-event decathlon. Beneath the rainy sky of the first day, Jim placed second in the 100-meter dash, the long jump, and the shot put. The next day, he won the high jump and the 110-meter hurdles, and finished second in the 400-meter race and the discus throw. On the final day, he placed third in the pole vault, fourth in the javelin, and then won the 1500-meter run. His combined score won him the decathlon and set a world record that would stand for sixteen years. One writer said that Jim's victory seemed "as easy as picking strawberries out of a dish." King Gustav of Sweden presented Jim with the gold medal. Later, Jim would say, "That was the proudest moment of my life."

Jim returned to Carlisle and football. That year, the team beat nearly everyone, including West Point's Army team. Their halfback, future president Dwight Eisenhower, said of Jim, "[Thorpe] was able to do everything that anyone else could, but he could do it better."

Jim was again voted onto the All-American team.

Then in 1913 a newspaper revealed that Jim had played baseball for money—a scandal, since the Olympic competition then banned professional athletes. Pop Warner advised Jim to confess. In a letter to the American Athletic Union, administrators of the American amateur athletes, he wrote: "I did not play for the money . . . but because I like to play ball. I am not wise in the ways of the world and did not realize that this (playing baseball for money) was wrong, and it would make me a professional in track sports."

Despite his explanation, the AAU decided to strip Jim of his medals and return them to the Olympic Committee. Jim's name was stricken from the Olympic records.

Jim was a proud man, and we can only guess at the humiliation he felt. "They used me as a guinea pig to make up the rules," he would later remark.

In 1913, Jim left Carlisle for good to play baseball for the New York Giants. Despite his high pay, $6,000 a year, it was an unhappy decision and he spent most of the time on the bench. But he liked the game and played for various major and minor league teams into the 1920s. Professional football also beckoned. In 1915, Jim played for the Canton Bulldogs, earning $250 a game. More clubs followed, including the Oorang Indians, made up of Native Americans, and the New York Football Giants. Jim even played professional basketball. Finally in 1928, after playing football for the Chicago Cardinals, Jim retired from professional sports.

Professional baseball: Jim Thorpe at bat with the New York Giants.

Jim found work in Hollywood, mostly bit roles playing Indians. Odd jobs followed: security guard, bartender, ditchdigger. He served in the merchant marines. He married and divorced, married and divorced, and married yet again. He fathered eight children, to whom he tried to impart his enduring love for the outdoors, taking them hunting and fishing. On March 28, 1953, while living in a trailer in Lomita, California, Jim Thorpe died of a heart attack. He was sixty-four years old.

Professional football: Jim Thorpe in uniform of the Canton, Ohio Bulldogs.

Jim's last wife, Patsy, insisted that a memorial be erected for Jim. She lobbied the state of Oklahoma, but no money was allotted for the project. In the end, Patsy convinced Mauch Chunk and East Mauch Chunk, two small towns in eastern Pennsylvania to which Jim had no connection, to pay for a memorial and rename the combined towns *Jim Thorpe*. And so, that is where you can find Jim today, resting in an unremarkable memorial beside an ordinary road.

In 1973, the AAU restored Jim's amateur status. In 1982, the International Olympic Committee reinstated Jim's honors, and a year later presented replicas of Jim's gold medals to his children. The originals had been lost.

BIBLIOGRAPHIC NOTE

This account of Jim Thorpe's life and achievements is based primarily on the following sources:

Crawford, Bill. *All American: The Rise and Fall of Jim Thorpe*, Hoboken, NJ: John Wiley & Sons, 2005.

Gould, Stephen Jay. "The Athlete of the Century," *American Heritage*, October 1998 (vol. 49, number 6, page 14).

Nardo, Don. *The Importance of Jim Thorpe*, San Diego, CA: Lucent Books, 1994.

Newcombe, Jack. *The Best of the Athletic Boys*, Garden City, NY: Doubleday & Company, 1975.

Wheeler, Robert W. *Jim Thorpe: World's Greatest Athlete*, Norman, OK: University of Oklahoma Press, 1975.

Descriptions of childhood, life outdoors, hunting, and farming are based on Thorpe's personal reminiscence, quoted by Wheeler (pages 8-14). On his feelings about school, Wheeler reports the testimony of Thorpe's childhood friend, Art Wakolee: "I knew Jim was not happy in school. . . . We got a licking many a time" (12). Newcombe quotes a Haskell teacher's characterization of Thorpe as a "restless child uninterested in anything but outdoor life" (43).

Of Hiram Thorpe, Jim's son Jack said, "I talked with my uncles and they all said everyone was afraid of Hiram. The only one that could stand up to him was Jim. Hiram could scare anyone in the county, but he couldn't control Dad" (Crawford, 22). Jim's daughter Grace described Hiram as a "horse breeder, wife-beater, and the strongest man in the county" (Crawford, 9,10). Of the "thrashing" that led to his running away in 1901, Jim recalled, "I deserved [it] but didn't feel like taking it. So I ran away from home to the Texas Panhandle." On returning, "My father took a look at the horses and decided to let me stay" (Wheeler, 18).

On Thorpe's move to Carlisle, both Crawford and Newcombe reprint a December 1903 letter from Hiram Thorpe to a U.S. Indian agent: "Dear Sir— I have boy that I wish you would make rangements to send of to school some ware. Carlisle r Hampton I don't care ware. . . ." Wheeler reports that a Carlisle recruiter approached Thorpe while he was at Haskell. Crawford, Newcombe, and Wheeler all describe Jim's unhappiness at Carlisle. Of Carlisle's system of sending students out to work on farms, Newcombe says that Thorpe felt "humiliated" and "increasingly mutinous" about it. Crawford cites Carlisle records showing Thorpe back at Carlisle within days of being sent out to a farm, and quotes a letter home from another Sac and Fox student, Sadie Ingalls: "I am sorry to say that JT is in the guard house for running away from his county home" (61).

Thorpe's personal recollection of breaking the Carlisle high-jump record is quoted in Wheeler (50). Various news accounts of the day describe Thorpe's abilities as a football player and his performance at the 1912 Olympic Games. The exchange between Thorpe and King Gustav of Sweden was recalled by the American gold medal-winning sprinter at the 1912 Olympics, Ralph Craig (Wheeler, 110, 296).

There is some confusion as to Thorpe's birth date. According to his estate and the Jim Thorpe website (www.cmgww.com/sports/thorpe/faq.htm), he was born May 28, 1887. Thorpe himself told the *Shawnee News Star* that he was born in 1888 (Wheeler, 291), and the Jim Thorpe memorial in Jim Thorpe, Pennsylvania, gives his birth date as 1888.